How to Make $2,000 a Month Online

50 ways to make money online with no formal training

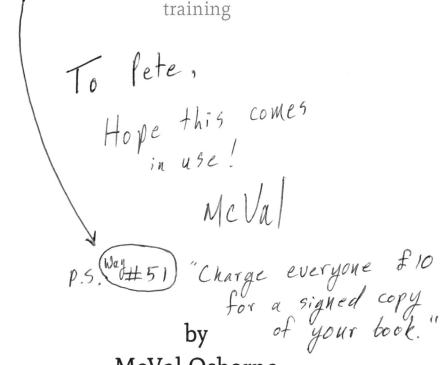

To Pete,
Hope this comes in use!
McVal

p.s. (Way #51) "Charge everyone £10 for a signed copy of your book."

by
McVal Osborne

Copyright © 2018 McVal Osborne
All rights reserved.

All rights reserved. No part of this book may be reproduced in any form without written permission from the author. Reviewers may quote brief passages in reviews.

Disclaimer and FTC Notice

No part of this book may be reproduced or transmitted in any form or by any means, electronic or mechanical, including photocopying, recording, faxing, emailing, posting online or by any information storage and retrieval system, without written permission from the author.

While all attempts have been made to verify the information provided in this publication, neither the author nor the publisher assumes any responsibility for errors, omissions, or contrary interpretations of the subject matter herein.

This book is for entertainment purposes only. The views expressed are those of the author alone, and should not be taken as expert instruction or commands. The reader is responsible for his or her own actions.

Adherence to all applicable laws and regulations, including international, federal, state, and local governing professional licensing, business practices, advertising and all other aspects of doing business in the US, Canada, or any other jurisdiction is the sole responsibility of the purchaser or reader.

Neither the author nor the publisher assumes any responsibility or liability whatsoever on the behalf of the purchaser or reader of these materials.

Any perceived slight of any individual or organization is purely unintentional.

I sometimes use affiliate links in the content. This means if you decide to make a purchase, I will get a sales commission. But that doesn't mean my opinion is for sale. Every affiliate link I include is for products I've personally used and found useful. Please do your own research before making any purchase online.

What Will You Do With Extra An $2,000 Every Month?

Go on vacation?

Buy a new car?

Put a down payment on a house?

Pay off student loans?

Invest in stocks?

Launch a new business?

Making money online may at first seem like an easy process: You come up with an idea for something to sell (an eBook, a gadget, a course), you make a website to sell it on, and then without so much as blinking an eye you start to see the money pour into your bank account.

I've got news for you, it ain't that easy.

The truth of the matter is, making money online is hard. It requires planning, focus and determination.

Sure, there are loads of tools, resources and courses out there to teach you how to create massive amounts of passive income overnight, but the vast majority of them will be useless to you unless you put in the work. Most "get rich quick" schemes are just that, schemes.

The people who are able to make real money online understand the balance between planning and execution. On top of that, they know how to leverage what they're already good at to start making money right away, rather than spending years trying to get good at something that will make them money later on.

The good news is that there are certain ways to increase the likelihood of achieving online money-making success. Today there are tons of online digital platforms available that make it possible to turn almost any skill, idea, product or service into cold, hard cash. Learn how to use these tools effectively and you'll be raking it in before you know it.

What you're about to read is a collection of 50 online freelancing and business ideas that are proven to bring in money and that require little to no skill, formal training, or investment up front.

Each idea is a separate strategy which, if executed properly, has the potential to make at least $2,000 a month using online tools while working less than 20 extra hours per week.

These ideas are used by entrepreneurs, digital nomads and side hustlers to build micro-businesses and freelancing gigs for fun and profit. While they aren't ideas that will make you rich overnight, they can provide you that buffer to set aside a little bit more money for that vacation or that down payment on a house. Since starting research on this book in October 2017, I have spoken with over 20 digital nomads and entrepreneurs to unpack their secrets on what it takes to create a successful side hustle. I've also personally tested at least five micro-business ideas described in this book and have increased my monthly side-hustle income to approximately $2,000 over the last 6 months.

The best part?

I didn't spend a lot of time on marketing or overthinking any of these side hustles. Instead, I chose one idea at a time and went for it. From there, the momentum of the idea carried me forward or it ground to a halt – which happened on more than one occasion. I was then able to start up on the next idea.

Making a few thousand dollars a month online in addition to your day job or as a side project doesn't have to be hard. Passive income experts and "side hustle gurus" love to over complicate the processes they use to achieve success and talk about how you need to spend weeks writing a business plan or hundreds of dollars advertising your products via social media to gain traction before you see a profit. In my opinion, this is a waste of time. The quicker you're able to get a gig, sign a contract, or deliver a product, the better.

What you're about to read are 50 ideas that have inspired me and continue to inspire entrepreneurs, digital nomads, and side hustlers in their search for financial flexibility. Each of these can help you make a start towards reaching financial independence, and perhaps will allow you to leave the 9 to 5 grind all together.

Table of Contents

What Will You Do With Extra An $2,000 Every Month? 6

Living the Dream One Experience at a Time 11

The idea behind How to Make $2,000 a Month Online 15

Trends in Remote Work 18

50 Ways to Make Money 21

    Sales (#1-6) 22

    Technology (#7-15) 35

    Human Connection (#16-24) 54

    Arts & Entertainment (#25-29) 73

    Strategy (#30-35) 83

    Operations (#36-43) 95

    Writing (#44-50) 111

Online Money Making Tools & Resources [Bonus Section] 126

    Remote jobs 126

    Freelance jobs 128

A Big Thank You 130

You don't have to try all 50 ideas. In fact, I would caution against it. This is simply a list of ideas that I hope will inspire you, as they have inspired me, to start thinking about how to earn a little bit of extra money on the side in your journey towards greater economic and personal freedom. In this book you'll get a good sense of the types of gigs that are available to you, and you will start to understand how you might leave the grind for good.

Excited yet?

Awesome! Let's jump right in.

Living the Dream One Experience at a Time

Imagine waking up in a cabana on the beach in Sri Lanka one morning. The sun is bright, and there isn't a cloud in the sky. It's 10am or thereabouts (you don't really wear a watch anymore) and you walk down the small hill where your cabana sits perched along a path to your hostel common area.

The owner of the establishment comes over and serves you fresh blended fruit juice, eggs, toast and coffee. You listen to the tropical birds call out in the distance and the howl of monkeys in the trees behind the bungalow. You look out and contemplate your workload as the waves crash about 50 feet in front of you.

You flip open your laptop and log on to the high speed WiFi that runs through the property. You check your Upwork and Fiverr accounts for any new jobs and notice 5 copywriting jobs that have come in overnight.

One is a rush job from Upwork that needs to be completed by tomorrow, a few chapters for someone's eBook, for which the fee will be $500.

The other four jobs are from Fiverr and are much smaller, but can be finished any time in the next week, $100 each. You've just made about $900 from a few jobs and about 15 hours of work.

Your hostel costs $20 per night ($140 per week, or $560 a month), which means you've got more than enough left over for food, drink and excursions around the island in addition to your room and board. Heck you might even decide to save some for a rainy day.

You may stay here a week and then go somewhere else, or you could decide to stay for a few months to really soak up the culture. Whatever you do, you know that you'll be able to rely on your digital revenue streams to keep you afloat even when things don't go exactly as planned.

This scenario is a made up one, but it could very easily play out for you in less time than you might think. The future is bright for the location independent entrepreneurs, the side hustlers and the digital nomads of this world. Before you know it, you could be one of the thousands of aspiring explorers and adventurers out there, looking to build a lifestyle and a business for yourself which supports your needs while helping you achieve a new type of success.

Entrepreneurs, digital nomads and side hustlers are changing the way the world works. The gig economy is alive and well, and every day traditional employees are leaving the workforce in search of more. More meaning, more money, more engagement. They are the new deep thinkers, life hackers and spiritual seekers, similar to the explorers of the past, and they are on a path to redefine what it means to be successful in this modern technological age.

But what's this all about?

Why are people making this change now?

I'll give you a hint, *it's all about experience.*

Think about it. You could just as easily live this life somewhere in Europe, Southeast Asia, Africa or South America. You can continue to earn money in a strong currency while travelling to countries where the economy is not as strong.

You can rely on a growing list of tools, networks and systems in place to support travelers and remote workers, and you can develop a lasting network of friends that will completely change the way you think about travel, society and the world as a whole.

You can have everything you want out of life, and you can travel the world at the same time. Just because you travel doesn't mean you should give up the idea of owning a home, starting a family, or settling down eventually. On the contrary. It is in this time of exploration that you can discover what you really want. Coming to terms with who you are through travel and exploration is one of the best ways to do that.

The life of the digital nomad is one that allows you to go anywhere and do anything your heart desires. It allows you utter flexibility, and at the same time security in the knowledge that you can support yourself and fend for yourself when times get tough. We currently live in a society that is, for the most part, relatively safe.

In every century prior to this one, danger lurked around every corner while travelling, and while some corners of the globe might not be incredibly safe at the moment, the ability to connect with anyone at any point on earth has truly given us a sense of global understanding and security. It is with this tool that you can build a real digital nomad lifestyle.

There are several reasons that the life of the digital nomad has become so popular in recent years. Among them, trends in demographics which indicate that more and more young people are choosing to embrace flexible working, remote working and contract work.

It is in these instances that you can see the growing number of flexible workers is something that will not only change the face of the future workforce, it will change the face of the globe as we know it.

The idea behind How to Make $2,000 a Month Online

Approximately 57.3 million Americans (36% of the U.S. workforce) freelanced in 2017 and most of the U.S. workforce will freelance by 2027. While freelancing is by no means a new form of making a living, the increasing popularity of freelancing makes it an attractive way for individuals to develop flexible, lifestyle businesses that support their needs around travel and adventure.

When I thought about how to come up with a list of top ways to develop a location independent lifestyle or freelance business (i.e. the life of a "Digital Nomad"), I settled on a few criteria we would use to offer selections and recommendations.

1. Minimal investment. You should be able to pick up and start these jobs with minimal investment in time or money. I would consider minimal investments to be less than $500, though if you need to purchase a new laptop, phone, camera, etc. those costs may rise quickly. I also considered the difference between an investment in hard costs (computer, camera, etc.) versus skills (training, coaching, etc.). If you require additional training to develop the skills required to complete a certain task, I have outlined either free or very cheap (<$500) courses available online which will allow you to get started. In some instances where certification is required by law the cost of this training may be much more.

2. Location independent. It would be possible to do this job remotely with a strong internet connection, a laptop, and an international phone plan. While there are plenty of jobs that require you to be in a specific location while travelling the world (e.g. hostel worker, fruit picker, etc.), I am not covering these jobs in this book. The reason for this is because I think that your ability to earn money remotely, wherever you are, is integral to your ability to develop the lifestyle of your dreams. You should not be required to time your travels or trips based on the weather or the availability of work in certain seasons.

3. Strong demand. I looked at jobs that are currently in high demand for freelancers according to sites such as Fiverr and Upwork. Most of these jobs require that you have highly technical skills before getting started. It is possible to develop these skills with time, but it will require dedicated effort. I have also identified jobs that allow you to start work right away while improving your skills over time. These jobs may be lower paid, but they are nevertheless in demand and may lead to more lucrative opportunities over time.

4. Well paid. Jobs on this list will allow you to make at least $2,000 per month while working less than 20-30 hours a week. While this doesn't mean you'll be splashing out on a yacht or a Maserati any time soon, you will be able to survive on the road with this earned income (especially if you choose to travel to less expensive countries).

5. Success is probable. I've chosen jobs where there is plenty of evidence that people working in these areas as freelancers can live comfortably while travelling and working remotely. I have spoken with individuals who have done this type of work, or I have spoken with experts that know it is possible. I put all these criteria through this lens to validate my own assumptions about which opportunities were best before sending them your way.

These criteria were selected because I feel the way in which you choose to live already requires taking risks. I would like to take as much of the guesswork out of how you decide to make a living as possible, which is why I've written this book.

While it may seem like a scary jump to make right now, rest assured that this is the opportunity of a lifetime. You will never be in the same place or time as you are right here in this moment, and if you feel the time is right you should dive in and take the plunge to create a new and vibrant life for yourself.

Trends in Remote Work

What do you think about when you hear the words remote worker, location independent entrepreneur, digital nomad, or side hustler?

Do you imagine a lonely writer or computer programmer, shut in her room, cranking out text or code for some nameless clients? Or do you imagine the attractive, charismatic explorer, travelling around the world while managing her business from a laptop and phone, effortlessly making contacts and connections along the way?

If you're like me, you imagine the latter. For many, the attraction of remote work is the ability to connect, interact and share stories with one another around the world. It is about freedom, yes, but it is also about developing a lifestyle which allows you to tap into higher levels of understanding and fulfillment across a wider spectrum.

The internet is full of articles, websites, blogs and stories about remote workers that quit their jobs to live the life of their dreams while gallivanting from place to place without a care in the world. Unfortunately, the reality of the matter is that the process of becoming a remote worker (or digital nomad) requires a lot of hard work and determination. Getting to a point where you can work remotely and be secure in your finances takes time and effort, and many people give up along the way when times get tough.

It is easy to imagine the positives and negatives of remote work if you spend any time thinking about it. In terms of flexibility, working remotely is top notch. You can travel when you want, work when you want, and connect with who you want. But it does come with drawbacks. There is the potential for loneliness or financial hardships. Many of those who take the plunge and dive into the world of remote work also find that they are less able to disconnect their personal and work lives. Emerging trends indicate this will get better and easier over time, so for now let's explore what is happening to make remote work more straightforward and what the future holds for people looking to cut ties with the regular office job.

Below are five emerging trends around changing worker behaviors and emerging technologies which are shifting the way work gets done:

Flexibility in a global economy becomes paramount. Today, even small companies can have a global footprint. With this trend, the need for real time communication from different time zones and regions is becoming more important.

Co-working and collaboration tech continues to grow in popularity. Increased numbers of people are opting for in-person co-working environments, even if they've stopped working in a traditional office space. Simultaneously, more companies are providing tools which allow people to collaborate online through the use of subscription platforms and services. Both in-person co-working and online collaboration platforms will continue to disrupt the traditional work space in the years ahead.

Professional social media goes mainstream. Professional interactions and relationships are being formed and strengthened using social media. Platforms such as LinkedIn and Slack are becoming universal and are changing the way in which businesses market to one another and communicate internally.

Management through artificial intelligence moves ahead. Automation of management and supervising tasks will become commonplace over the next 10 years, and individuals that learn to leverage these tools will be much better placed to manage relationships with clients and suppliers while working remotely.

Technology skills become table stakes. It's more important than ever for workers in all industries and across all levels to keep their tech skills up to date and on the cutting edge. This is especially true for remote workers and digital nomads, who are responsible for keeping their talents up to date to keep attracting work. Those who don't have the most up to date skills risk losing out on important contracts and will be forced to change their approach to work.

In conclusion, we live in a world which is changing rapidly. People need a push to question what they want, but at the same time appreciate what they need out of their work and their business in order to thrive. Remote work may not be for everyone, but it can be a straightforward process for those who do want to give it a try. I would urge anyone that is interested in taking a leap in this direction to give it a try, because you never know where you may end up.

50 Ways to Make Money

While it is easy to brain dump a bunch of ideas on how to make money online, I still needed to find examples of people that have done all of the suggestions in this book. I needed to find proof that these jobs have been done by people remotely as side hustles and that there was a relatively strong demand for the products or services in question. What follows is a list of 50 ideas for earning money online, backed up by evidence and bucketed into certain specific areas:

- Sales (affiliate marketing, B2B sales)
- Technology (programming, coding, developing)
- Human Connection (brand, consulting, coaching, teaching)
- Arts & Entertainment (design, art, audio, video)
- Strategy (product development, innovation planning, market research, business plan writing)
- Operations (project management, data entry, interviewing)
- Writing (freelance writing, blogging, copywriting, content generation)

Sales (#1-6)

"Approach each customer with the idea of helping him or her to solve a problem or achieve a goal, not of selling a product or service."
– Brian Tracy

I often hear people say, I would love to be an entrepreneur, I just hate sales. Unfortunately for them, very few entrepreneurs will manage to succeed in their ventures unless they develop some type of marketing or sales skill.

Sales requires enthusiasm, organization, and a deep connection with the customer. Salespeople need to be empathetic and understanding, and they also must be able to put themselves in the shoes of those who they help.

Some people are born for sales. They're outgoing, love talking to people, and tend to be creative thinkers that are eager for a challenge. If this sounds like you, you might want to consider one of these ideas.

1. Affiliate marketing

Difficulty: Medium
Profit Potential: Medium
Size of Opportunity: Large
Initial Cost: Low

What is it?
Affiliate marketing is when you get paid to market and sell other people's products. When you find a product that you think you can sell, you arrange a deal with the company in question and receive a percentage commission for each product they sell that comes directly from the unique link that they give you. Driving sales through the creation of links to specific products is one of the easiest ways to get started with creating real income online. There are many people out there creating massive amounts of passive income from this type of system.

How much can I make?
The upside for affiliate marketing is that you don't hold any inventory or need to purchase any products ahead of time, making it very inexpensive to get started. It's hard to estimate how much you will make on affiliate marketing, but there are numerous examples of marketers making upwards of $6,000 to $8,000 PER DAY in affiliate marketing depending on their marketing tactics and strategies. For that reason, I think reaching the $2,000 per month target isn't unreasonable.

How do I start?
There are plenty of resources for people looking to learn how to develop their skills in affiliate marketing. Two of my favorites are Clickbank and CJ Affiliate.

Skills Needed
- Marketing skills and creativity
- Problem solving and critical thinking
- Technical expertise in affiliate links

Digital Resources
- **About Affiliate Marketing:** Charles Ngo's blog on affiliate marketing is a fantastic resource for those interested in learning more about this side hustle (https://charlesngo.com/).
- **Terraleads**: The world's first CPA Hub and a direct advertiser of nutra offers represented in the following categories: beauty, diet, health, and adult.
- **Clickbank**: One of the largest affiliate networks online with over 1.5 million affiliates and 6 million clients.
- **CJ By Conversant**: CJ Affiliate is an online marketing and affiliate advertising company owned by Alliance Data, formerly known as Commission Junction.
- **Rakuten**: A global affiliate network processing payments in over 200 countries.
- **Amazon Associates**: Over 1 million products from the Amazon store to advertise to potential customers. Earn 10% in advertising fees. One of the first online affiliate marketing programs and was launched in 1996.

2. Inside sales / virtual sales assistant

Difficulty: Hard
Profit Potential: High
Size of Opportunity: Medium
Initial Cost: Low

What is it?
A growing number of big companies are looking to grow their inside sales teams by operating a remote salesforce. If you are a strong sales person, consider becoming a sales person for a company that has products or services you believe in.

Many companies are open to the idea of hiring outside sales people that earn based on commission. The role of a salesperson requires focus and dedication, so you should be aware that you may be required to pick up the phone and call prospective clients at bizarre times if you are living in a remote location and are in a different time zone. Remote sales work can be alluring and lucrative, and all it requires is determination and hard work.

How much can I make?
Becoming a virtual sales agent can be incredibly lucrative, especially if you are working with a product that you believe in and can speak about in a way that shows the value to the potential customer.

Sales in this type of role can be incredibly varied. I've spoken with sales professionals working remotely for the market research industry (selling surveys to large corporations), selling construction and architectural design software to construction firms, or even selling sales tools to fashion brands.

Most of the time this work relates to sales of information products or software solutions, and it is frequently done in a business to business

(B2B) context. Very few virtual sales roles require selling directly to a customer, unless it is a very high value product (think Rolex watches, timeshares or super yachts).

As a virtual travel agent, you typically start with a low base salary and make commission based on what you sell. This can often be more than double or triple the base salary. You decide how much you work and for how long.

If you are able to work efficiently, you can make a comfortable income (around $2,000 to $5,000 per month) working 15-20 hours per week. All you need is an international calling plan through a service like Skype or Zoom and a strong internet connection.

How do I start?
Go to websites like gumtree or indeed.com to find a whole list of job postings for virtual or remote sales agents.

Skills Needed
- Proficient computer, analytical, decision-making, and organizational skills
- Strong interpersonal and persuasive skills in order to communicate effectively with customers and prospects
- Strong multitasking and typing capabilities

Digital Resources
- **Indeed.com**: Directory of job postings from around the world, but predominantly in the US. Search specifically for "remote inside executive" jobs to find several thousand sales jobs that allow for remote work.
- **Remote.co**: Directory of remote jobs around the world, searchable by sales role.

3. Dropship products on Amazon

Difficulty: Medium
Profit Potential: Low
Size of Opportunity: Medium
Initial Cost: Medium

What is it?
Fulfilled by Amazon (FBA) is a platform managed by Amazon that allows sellers to start and run businesses selling physical products without ever seeing those products in person. If you would like to become part of the largest marketplace for products on earth, consider opening a store for physical products on Amazon and selling through FBA. Starting a business on Amazon may sound daunting, but it doesn't have to be.

How much can I make?
Depending on the product and the niche you decide to focus on, Amazon FBA entrepreneurs can make anywhere from $1,000 to $2,500 a month selling products online which require little to no day-to-day upkeep.

How do I start?
Start by visiting the Amazon FBA website. There are plenty of guides and resources online for how to start selling through FBA, and there are loads of success stories of people who have managed to leave their corporate jobs and join the next generation in entrepreneurs (the group that Tim Ferriss refers to as the "new rich") in their search for income automation and autonomy.

Skills Needed
- Organization and attention to detail
- Communication and negotiation skills
- Tech and financial knowledge

Digital Resources
- **FBA "How it Works" by Amazon**: Easy how-to guide for getting started with Amazon FBA (https://services.amazon.com/fulfillment-by-amazon/how-it-works.html).
- **Startup Bros Guide**: If this route interests you, consider starting with the rigorously thought through guide developed by StartupBros (https://startupbros.com/how-to-sell-on-amazon-fba/).

4. Private label products on Amazon

Difficulty: Hard
Profit Potential: High
Size of Opportunity: Medium
Initial Cost: High

What is it?
When you private label a product, it means that you take a product that has been manufactured by someone else (typically in China) and you slap your own logo on it. You can also take an existing product and modify it slightly to make it your own. The benefit of doing this is that you can create your own brand around the products that you sell and manufacture, and you can charge a premium for those products. The risk is that you have to invest more up front to design a logo and order a certain amount of inventory with your logo on it.

How much can I make?
The margins for products in this category tend to be higher than for those who just sell other manufacturer's products without a private label. Successful entrepreneurs that start private label businesses can make anywhere from $5,000 to $15,000 a month selling products online.

How do I start?
Start by doing a bit of digging online. If you're interested in going down this route, there are plenty of entrepreneurs that do this very well. One of my favorites is Riley Bennett, who I spoke to from his home base in Chiang Mai, Thailand.

Skills Needed
- Organization, attention to detail, and creativity
- Communication and negotiation skills
- Tech and financial knowledge

Digital Resources
- Check out the videos produced by Riley Bennett on his YouTube channel Living That Life. (http://livinthatlife.com/)

5. Etsy

Difficulty: Medium
Profit Potential: Low
Size of Opportunity: Medium
Initial Cost: Low

What is it?
Etsy is a fantastic website for creatives to make money from their artistic endeavors. Etsy is an ecommerce website that focuses on consumer-to-consumer sales of handmade and vintage products. Etsy differentiates itself through the unique products available on its site which aren't found anywhere else. It has a loyal customer base made up of long time returning customers. The site was launched in 2005 and has attracted artists and makers from around the world.

How much can I make?
The average Etsy seller makes around $700 a month selling products through the site. While this doesn't meet the $2,000 we set in our initial business idea search criteria, there is room to grow this type of business into something larger.

How do I start?
If you've got a creative streak and like making things with your hands, it's worth considering starting an Etsy shop. The best way to start is to visit the Etsy website and build a profile for your first store.

Skills Needed
- Creativity
- Persistence
- Passion

Digital Resources
- **Etsy Seller Handbook**: Resource list of articles to help you launch the best Etsy store (https://www.etsy.com/uk/seller-handbook)
- **Udemy**: Udemy has several courses to help you optimize your Etsy store for SEO and improve things like photos, listing text, and product categories.

6. Ebay

Difficulty: Low
Profit Potential: Medium
Size of Opportunity: Low
Initial Cost: Low

What is it?
If you don't know what eBay is by now, you may have been living under a rock for most of the early 2000s. eBay is an ecommerce platform for consumer-to-consumer sales of new and used products. It has over 14,000 employees and regularly records revenues over $9 billion USD.

To make money on eBay, users from around the world post things they have purchased with a brief description. Each listing can be targeted to a specific region or sold internationally.

How much can I make?
You can easily make $2,000 or more on eBay depending on what you're selling and how you market your products. Traditionally, sellers that sell niche products are more successful than those who sell commodities.

How do I start?
There are loads of training courses on YouTube and Udemy as well as loads of blogs and articles which describe different best practices and ways to create a profitable eBay business

Skills Needed
- Organizational skills
- Attention to detail

Digital Resources
- **eBay:** Sell an item - Getting Started (https://pages.ebay.co.uk/help/sell/sell-getstarted.html)
- **Udemy:** eBay Drop Shipping Guide (https://www.udemy.com/ebay-drop-shipping-guide-with-no-inventory-work-from-home/)

Technology (#7-15)

"Technology is anything that wasn't around when you were born."
Alan Kay

We live in a world ruled by digital technology. In every waking moment we use technology. We communicate with others, track our personal progress, do business, or find out what's going on somewhere else in the world. Technology has become the oxygen we breathe, an absolutely necessity to do what we do every day. Whether we like it or not, we live and die by the smartphones in our pockets.

Every year, more and more people start location independent businesses or decide to work remotely with the help of technology. It is because of technology centric jobs like the ones listed here that we are able to build online ecommerce platforms and create streamlined mobile apps for sharing photos or order taxis.

If you have an interest in learning to program or already have some experience in a more technical area of work, consider going with one of these ideas. There is still a massive shortage of skilled tech workers, and it is relatively easy to make a good side income from many of these jobs with a little bit of effort.

7. Personalized ecommerce site (Shopify / Wix)

Difficulty: Medium
Profit Potential: Medium
Size of Opportunity: Medium
Initial Cost: Low

What is it?
While you may not want to dive in to start your own ecommerce website right away, what's to stop you from making some money creating sites for other people? If you've got some tech knowledge and an interest in website development, you may want to start selling your capabilities to build ecommerce sites for other aspiring entrepreneurs.

How much can I make?
On Upwork, eCommerce website developers charge between $75 and $100 an hour for website creation and support. This means only working an extra 5-7 hours per week (20-30 hours a MONTH) to make around $2,000 in extra income.

How do I start?
If you want to start a job consulting as an eCommerce website developer, consider exploring a few how to courses on YouTube. Beyond that, the best way to get comfortable with these platforms is to practice. Go sign up for free trials on Shopify and Wix to test your skills before creating an account on Upwork and Fiverr. Once you create an account on either of these sites, put your price point low at first to get a few good reviews before raising it up to the $100/hr rate.

Skills Needed
- Tech savvy
- Basic understanding of coding, programming
- WordPress, website design

Digital Resources
- **WP Beginner:** How to Start an Online Store (https://www.wpbeginner.com/wp-tutorials/how-to-start-an-online-store/)
- **Shopify:** Create an Ecommerce Website (https://www.shopify.co.uk/tour/ecommerce-website)
- **Wix:** Create an eCommerce Website (https://www.wix.com/)

8. Website design

Difficulty: Medium
Profit Potential: High
Size of Opportunity: Large
Initial Cost: Medium

What is it?
Web design platforms like Squarespace, Wix and WordPress have made it incredibly easy to create beautiful websites in little to know time. If you have an eye for design and an understanding of one or more of these platforms, you will be in a good position to sell your skills in website design.

How much can I make?
Website designers can make between $40-100/hr on Upwork. Simple websites might take between 20 and 40 hours to create. Web designers could potentially make anywhere from $800 to $4,000 per site.

How do I start?
Be sure to create a few template websites as practice to show other people before you start pitching your skills on Fiverr and Upwork.

Skills Needed
- Programming or coding (HTML5, CSS)
- Experience with WordPress, Square, Wix

Digital Resources
- **uDemy:** Beginner Website Creation (https://www.udemy.com/learn-wordpress-website-creation-web-design/)
- **Wix:** 10 Essential Tutorials That Every Wix Newbie Should Know (https://www.wix.com/blog/2016/11/10-wix-essential-tutorials/)
- **Squarespace:** How to create a website on Squarespace (https://www.squarespace.com/)

9. Blog management

Difficulty: Medium
Profit Potential: High
Size of Opportunity: Medium
Initial Cost: Low

What is it?
There are over 300 million blogs online today. The vast majority of them are poorly managed or not updated frequently enough, which means there is a massive opportunity for digital nomads to help businesses streamline their blogs and help drive traffic to their websites. If you have any experience with WordPress or other blog and web design platforms, consider advertising your management and planning skills to help other businesses and entrepreneurs manage their blogs and online social profiles. A well managed blog is more likely to attract traffic and help grow the business of whoever owns it, so it is in the best interest of blog owners to have their blogs managed by someone who has experience in this area.

How much can I make?
Most business people are also quite busy and don't want to regularly update these blogs. Thankfully, the process of managing a blog and keeping it up to date can take as little as a few hours a week, and you can charge upwards of $500 per month per client for this type of service. If you have 4-6 blogs that you manage, this could mean a regular paycheck of $2,000 to $3,000 per month, for as little as 12 hours of work per week. Not too bad.

How do I start?
Take a look at what other blog managers are doing on Upwork and Fiverr to see if you can copy their style and approach. These sites will be the best place to start looking for traffic, but you will want to

expand your client list by getting references from those clients you get on Upwork.

Skills Needed
- Time management
- Client management
- Project management

Digital Resources
- **The Minimalist:** A great resource for individuals looking to start and manage a blog (https://www.theminimalists.com/blog/)
- **All Blogging Tips:** This is a fantastic source of information on the business behind running a blog (https://allbloggingtips.com/blogging-is-a-business-how-to-start-run-and-operate-your-blog-it-matters/)
- **Pro Blogger:** Perhaps my favorite blogging how-to site. Check out this specific blog post on how to make money while blogging (https://problogger.com/make-money-blogging/)

10. Graphic design

Difficulty: High
Profit Potential: Medium
Size of Opportunity: Medium
Initial Cost: Medium

What is it?
Whether you're designing something for products, apps, websites, or something else, selling your skills at graphic design can be a great way to get regular work. UX design in particular is an area of growing interest for startups and small businesses looking to develop experiences for their customers which stand out from the pack. There are also loads of open source software tools that make graphic design and UX design something that can be picked up quite quickly.

How much can I make?
While it takes many years to become an expert in this area of work, you can start up quickly and start charging more over time. Expect to make at least $300 per day working 4-6 hours on designs through sites like Upwork or Fiverr.

How do I start?
Create a profile on Upwork or Fiverr. Also consider subscribing to design program like Adobe Creative Cloud and stock image sites.

Skills Needed
- Artistic eye, strong creativity
- Good communication and client facing ability
- Design programs like Adobe Creative Cloud
- Experience with stock image sites

Digital Resources
- **Adobe Creative Cloud:** Adobe's suite of subscription creative tools (https://www.adobe.com/uk/creativecloud.html)
- **Deposit Photos:** Stock photo site (http://www.depositphotos.com)

11. UX design

Difficulty: High
Profit Potential: High
Size of Opportunity: High
Initial Cost: Medium

What is it?
The rise of technology has meant the rise of the UX designer in fields related to tech development, especially in apps. User experience (UX) design is concerned with the look and feel of a product. Being a UX designer means working on the process of creating products that provide meaningful and relevant experiences to users. This means working with a client to design the entire process of creating the product, including aspects of branding, design, usability, and function.

How much can I make?
UX designers typically charge between $50-75/hr and can earn between $2,000 and $5,000 a month depending on the number of projects they have going.

How do I start?
UX design requires creativity and attention to detail. To start down the path of UX design, read as many blogs and reports on UX design as you can get your hands on. In addition to that, start working on fake projects and posting them on Dribbble, the main directory for finding and hiring UX designers.

Skills Needed
- Wireframing and UI prototyping
- Consumer empathy and good communication skills
- Creativity and artsy-ness

Digital Resources
- **Dribbble:** Directory for finding and hiring designers (https://dribbble.com/)
- **UX Design Weekly:** Fantastic source for weekly design articles curated by Kenny Chen (http://uxdesignweekly.com/)

12. Develop software

Difficulty: High
Profit Potential: Medium
Size of Opportunity: Medium
Initial Cost: High

What is it?
Computer programmers used to be seen as the nerdy kids sitting alone, working on a project as the cool kids went out to parties or travelled the world. This stereotype no longer holds much water, as more and more programmers and app developers are deciding to live and work remotely as virtual freelancers. As technology changes and shifts, there is an ever growing window of opportunity for people who are programmers to work remotely and make a great income while travelling. If you have programming skills and are interested in travelling, you are in a brilliant position to start working remotely.

Software development is the process through which an individual conceives of an idea for some piece of software, designs its features, programs the tool, documents everything and tests it to make sure it works. Software development is essential in today's society, especially as we rely more and more on technology to run and manage our lives. It is estimated that there are over 18 million software developers in the world today. This figure is estimated to increase to over 26 million by 2019, an increase of 45%.

How much can I make?
A quick search on Upwork reveals that most skills software engineers and developers that are making money regularly charge between $75 and $100/hr for their services. This may differ depending on your level of expertise, but it's a good line in the sand. Thus, working approximately 10 to 20 hours a week could feasibly make you between $4,000 and $8,000 in side income each month.

Developing software as a freelancer can be a lucrative side job, but without a team behind you to manage the full development process it can be challenging to create quality products in a timely manner. Most software developers and engineers work as contractors as part of a larger team.

How do I start?
If, like me, you are interested in learning how to code but have never done it before, there are plenty of resources out there which will help you reach a level where you can sell your services as a freelancer in as little as one month. In fact, there are several programs available through websites like Udemy and the website Onemonth.com (https://onemonth.com/) which provide specific boot-camp courses that help you perfect a certain skill in just 30 days, all for under $200 ($199 to be exact). Once you have even a basic understanding of certain programming languages and techniques, you are then well positioned to start earning upwards of $30 to 45 an hour on Upwork working on app creation or various types of development.

Skills Needed
- Knowledge of software development lifecycle
- Computer programming languages
- Attention to detail

Digital Resources
- **Udemy:** The Upwork site has plenty of computer programming and development courses available.
- **Code Academy:** Learn to code for free (https://www.codecademy.com/)
- **Code.org:** Fantastic resource for free coding courses (https://code.org/learn)
- **Code Mentor:** Great story of how Alex Kehaya learned how to program in 30 days

(https://www.codementor.io/afkehaya/learning-how-to-code-in-just-30-days-du107lnk4)
- **One Month:** Online course designed to teach you how to code in 30 days (https://onemonth.com/)

13. Social media management

Difficulty: Medium
Profit Potential: Medium
Size of Opportunity: Medium
Initial Cost: Low

What is it?
Having a social media presence is integral to small business success. Social media marketing is the heartbeat of online ecommerce, and it is one of the key ways that businesses attract leads. But many businesses lack the time to publish, post, and manage their social media accounts. Businesses all around the world are missing out on the opportunity for exposure.

Success comes from establishing a presence on Facebook, Instagram, Twitter, and Snapchat, but if businesses don't have the manpower or time to devote to social media then they have to hire someone to be their Social Media Manager.

How much can I make?
Social media managers can make between $40 to $60 per hour on social media marketing and account management. While social media management can require time consuming research up front, it is typically a low touch job which only requires a few hours a day per client (even less in some cases). If you are able to build up a client list of between 4-6 clients on an ongoing basis you can easily earn between $3,000 and $4,500 a month without breaking a sweat.

How do I start?
Start by doing your research into what it takes to manage social media accounts effectively. Check out thought leadership social media sites like NeilPatel.com. Review what tools are currently being used in the

marketplace (i.e. Hootsuite, SemRush, Sprout Social). Create a profile for yourself in Upwork and Fiverr and start pitching for jobs!

Skills Needed
- Organizational skills and time management
- Strong interpersonal skills
- Creativity and curiosity
- Empathy for different customer groups

Digital Resources
- **NeilPatel.com:** Neil Patel is one of the most well-respected social media gurus online, and his blog is one of the most well-read blogs on the subject of social media management and marketing out there (https://neilpatel.com/blog/)
- **WordStream:** Great blog on 7 Best Free Social Media Management Tools (https://www.wordstream.com/blog/ws/2018/01/17/best-free-social-media-management-tools)
- **Lyfe Marketing:** Awesome post on "What is Social Media Management?" (https://www.lyfemarketing.com/blog/what-is-social-media-management/)
- **Hootsuite:** One of my favorite free tools when it comes to social media management (https://hootsuite.com/)

14. Social media advertising

Difficulty: Medium
Profit Potential: High
Size of Opportunity: Medium
Initial Cost: Medium

What is it?
As a social media marketer or advertising specialist, you are responsible for managing and running social media marketing campaigns on platforms like Facebook, Twitter, Instagram and LinkedIn. This requires planning overarching campaign strategy, designing advertising content, creating content, launching advertising, and tracking results on ad tracking platforms.

Social media advertising is an increasingly important channel for businesses to use in their repertoire of resources for attracting customers and clients. Social media advertisers are expected to spend more than $50 billion on advertising on mobile and desktop ads in 2018, and that figure is expected to increase 10% each year.

How much can I make?
Social media advertisers make between $40 and $60 per hour depending on their level of experience on Upwork and Fiverr, similar to social media managers. This means you can likely make between $3,000 to $4,500 per month with a few clients working about 18-20 hours a week. As your skills improve, you may be able to earn much more than this with individual recommendations and referrals, but this gives you a place to start.

How do I start?
This is one of the jobs that may require specific training or additional expertise to provide quality services to customers. Look for courses online which provide specific training for certain platforms like

Instagram or Facebook advertising. I would recommend sticking with one media channel to start with. Once you've developed your skills in that channel, consider expanding into another social network.

Skills Needed
- Creative and enthusiastic
- Well organized and detail oriented
- Project management skills a plus

Digital Resources
- **Facebook Business:** 2 billion people use Facebook every month (https://www.facebook.com/business/products/ads)
- **Instagram Business:** One of the fastest growing social media marketing channels to date (https://business.instagram.com/advertising?)
- **Snapchat for Business:** Advertising for Snapchat (https://forbusiness.snapchat.com/)

15. Manage SEO

Difficulty: Medium
Profit Potential: Medium
Size of Opportunity: Medium
Initial Cost: Low

What is it?
As an SEO manager, you are responsible for making sure that a website's content is optimized for search engines like Google and Bing. Search engine optimisation is the process through which someone optimizes a website and its content so that it can easily be indexed by search engines.

How much can I make?
You can make between $50 and $100 depending on your level of expertise and how you position your work. There are dozens of SEO jobs posted on Fiverr and Upwork, which is good. That means there's a market for this type of work.

How do I start?
Get reading about SEO! The links below will provide a good starting point. From there, start practicing SEO on your own test site or program. Then create a profile on Fiverr and Upwork and start applying to jobs.

Skills Needed
- Technical knowledge of website design
- WordPress
- Writing

Digital Resources
- **Internet Marketing Ninjas:** "How to Become an SEO Expert" is a great blog post on how to go on the path of becoming an SEO expert (https://www.internetmarketingninjas.com/blog/career/how-to-become-an-seo-how-i-did-it-and-how-you-can-too/)
- **eConsultancy:** "What SEO Beginners Need to Know" is a great post on the basics of SEO (https://econsultancy.com/blog/64915-what-seo-beginners-need-to-know-a-basic-skills-guide)
- **NeilPatel.com:** I'll mention Neil Patel one more time in this section. He's a fantastic resource on all things internet marketing related, and loads of his content is around SEO optimization (https://neilpatel.com/blog/)

Human Connection (#16-24)

"Leaders lead when they take positions, when they connect with their tribes, and when they help the tribe connect to itself."
Seth Godin

Technology is changing the way humans interact with one another. Some of this is good, and some of it is bad. We are more connected than ever before from a technological standpoint, but we are arguably less connected with those around us. Human connection is something that we all crave, but it's not something that we all get. People want to feel appreciated, understood, and respected, yet in many instances we miss opportunities to connect and share these feelings with others.

There is a clear need for products and services that enable human connection and collaboration. We benefit from speaking to others about our ideas, talking through problems, and generally looking for solutions through combined efforts. If you want to make a difference in society while making some money, look for ways to leverage digital technology in one of these human connection side hustles.

16. Life coaching

Difficulty: Medium
Profit Potential: High
Size of Opportunity: Large
Initial Cost: Medium / High

What is it?
Life coaches provide guidance to people about how they think about goal setting and success. The popularity of life coaches in recent years has shot through the roof, and it is a fast growing and popular space. It is becoming increasingly more relevant as people realize they are growing more stressed and have less time to focus on what they want to do.

How much can I make?
Life coaches can earn anywhere from $50 to $500 an hour. Some coaches can demand much higher prices because of their expertise and their experience in different areas, but as you look to start out as a life coach you may want to commit to starting smaller. If you charge $50 an hour, you may be able to make as much as $2,000 per month by working around 10 hours per week. Most life coaches sell packages of 6 sessions at a time at a specific rate.

How do I start?
Because being a life coach currently requires no formalised training, you can launch a business in this space very quickly. People that succeed in this area have strong interpersonal skills and know how to help guide people towards better decision making and strategic thinking about what they want out of life.

Skills Needed
- Empathy
- Emotional intelligence
- Organization

Digital Resources
- **WikiHow:** How to Be a Life Coach (https://www.wikihow.com/Be-a-Life-Coach)
- **Life Coach Hub:** The Beginners Guide to Life Coaching (https://www.lifecoachhub.com/beginners-guide-to-life-coaching)
- **Huffington Post:** "Life Coach Certification: How to find the best program" (https://www.huffingtonpost.com/victoria-yore/life-coach-certification-_b_11409722.html)

17. Career counselling

Difficulty: Medium
Profit Potential: Medium
Size of Opportunity: Medium
Initial Cost: Low

What is it?
Few people know exactly what they want to do with their lives. They need support to understand their options and to help develop a plan to move towards. Deep down, most people have a good idea of what they want to do with their lives. What stands in their way are all the messages told to them by other people about why they can't or shouldn't pursue those goals. If you have experience talking to people about what they want to do with their lives, chances are you may find this a good way to develop a strong side business.

How much can I make?
Career coaches can aim to make somewhere between $50 to $100 per hour long Skype or FaceTime session to start off with. Be aware that, because you are targeting individuals who are looking to change the trajectory of their job and may be at an earlier stage in their career, they may be less willing to pay higher amounts.

How do I start?
There are several guides online for how to start your own career consulting and counselling business, and there are even a few networks that make this process very straightforward for both users and counsellors.

Skills Needed
- Emotional intelligence
- Patience and listening
- Resume writing

Digital Resources
- **WikiHow:** How to be a Career Coach (https://www.wikihow.com/Become-a-Career-Coach)
- **Udemy:** Lots of courses on career coaching available through Udemy.

18. Health and wellness coaching

Difficulty: Medium
Profit Potential: Medium
Size of Opportunity: Medium
Initial Cost: Low

What is it?
Health and wellness coaching is a rapidly growing area. Yoga instructors, nutritionists, mindfulness coaches and therapists are in more demand now than ever before. If you have an interest in healthy living (especially healthy living and wellness in a specific niche), consider starting a business where you write about and coach people in how to live a healthy and happy life.

How much can I make?
Health and wellness coaches can make anywhere from $50 to $100 per session, and typically sell packages of 6 sessions at a time.

How do I start?
The world is full of people that are too busy to find the time to take care of themselves, so health and wellness coaching is a valuable gift to be able to share with people if you have the interest in it. Look to sites like Thrive for inspirational content on health and wellness, and for ways to launch your own business in this space.

Skills Needed
- Compassion for others
- Passion for wellness and health sector
- Writing, filmmaking / editing a plus

Digital Resources
- **Health Coach Certifications:** "How much do Certified Health and Wellness Coaches Make?" (http://www.healthcoachcertifications.com/the-health-coach-salary-how-much-does-a-certified-health-and-wellness-coach-make-from-salary/)
- **Udemy:** Lots of courses on wellness coaching available through Udemy

19. Mindfulness coaching

Difficulty: Hard
Profit Potential: High
Size of Opportunity: Large
Initial Cost: Medium / High

What is it?
The World Health Organization (WHO) estimates that by 2030, mental health issues will be the biggest burden on health care resources in the world, surpassing heart conditions and cancer. While mental health is a broad ranging topic, there is growing interest in understanding how mental health, stress, and anxiety are related to the increased use of technology and the way we live our lives.

Mindfulness coaching and mindfulness-based stress-reduction (MBSR) has been growing in popularity recently because it offers a preventative solution to stress and anxiety. With the growth of technology platforms and the use of tools like Skype and FaceTime, mindfulness coaches can be anywhere in the world while connecting with their clients to help reduce stress and anxiety in their lives.

How much can I make?
Mindfulness coaches can make between $60-80 per hour working with individuals over Skype. Mindfulness coaches can also work with groups by running online workshops and teaching digital courses, which can lead to higher income.

How do I start?
Depending on where you are, you will need to carry out specific training to allow you to teach mindfulness to others. Look for Mindfulness Based Stress-Reduction(MBSR) Teacher Development Programs near you. Courses tend to be around 8 weeks and can cost between $1,500 and $2,500.

Skills Needed
- Compassion
- Emotional intelligence
- Focus

Digital Resources
- **Mindfulness Training Institute (U.S.):** The major mindfulness training body in the U.S., headquartered in San Francisco
- **British Mindfulness Institute (UK):** The UK equivalent of the Mindfulness Training Institute (https://www.britishmindfulnessinstitute.co.uk/portfolio-item/mbct-training/)
- **Teach Mindfulness Online:** One of the many mindfulness teacher training courses available online (http://teachmindfulnessonline.com/home/)

20. Online course creation for a specific work-related skill or self-improvement topic

Difficulty: Medium
Profit Potential: High
Size of Opportunity: Medium
Initial Cost: Medium / High

What is it?
This is a really fun one. The market for online courses and training is skyrocketing, as people are looking for ways to learn valuable skills online rather than spending a fortune going into the classroom.

How much can I make?
The amount of money you can make through an online course depends on the topic you choose to teach and the size of your audience. On Udemy, some instructors can make up to $5,000 a month from multiple courses, while others struggle to make $4,000 per year for a single course (about $300 per month). The name of the game here is to do your homework up front and spend the time to create the best course possible before launching.

How do I start?
Teaching online can be done in a variety of ways, through digital reports and workbooks in PDF to more intricate presentations delivered via video and customised online platforms like those offered on Udemy.

One thing to be aware of when considering the development of an online course is that it requires time up front to design and record the course, followed by marketing on the back end. If you are interested in going this route, I would recommend looking into tools such as Udemy and the online course building training called Create Awesome Online Courses.

Skills Needed
- Organization
- Enthusiasm for the topic
- Tech knowledge

Digital Resources
- **Udemy:** The largest online website for selling courses (https://www.udemy.com/)
- **Teachable:** Online training site similar to Udemy (https://teachable.com/)
- **Create Awesome Online Courses:** This course taught by David Siteman Garland is a fantastic place to get started before you create your own course (https://www.createawesomeonlinecourses.com/)

21. Develop an online training course for a specific certification or exam

Difficulty: Hard
Profit Potential: High
Size of Opportunity: Medium
Initial Cost: Medium

What is it?
There's no denying that online courses are growing in popularity. Courses that are developed specifically for a certain certification or exam are more likely to be popular and demand a high price because users are keen to solve a problem (e.g. pass a specific test or certification). If you have a certain expertise in an area that requires certification and you know how to help people get there quicker or more easily, create a course with this in mind.

How much can I make?
Courses like this tend to be of higher value than those on general topics and interest areas. You can likely charge a higher rate for these courses than you would others. You should be able to charge somewhere between $150 to $200 for a certification style course, meaning you only have to sell about 10 courses a month to meet your $2,000 per month target.

How do I start?
Think about how you can make a new training program for a specific test or certification exam which adds an additional layer of value or a different perspective. If you can do this, you will likely be able to attract a load of customers to your course. While having expertise in a certain area doesn't hurt, you shouldn't avoid this way of making money simply because you don't know about the topic. People regularly pay for synthesized and simplified information, so you should consider taking a more advanced topic and simplifying it for a busy audience. Use a

course creation platform like Udemy or Course Cats, or develop your own program via a personal website.

Skills Needed (same as for the previous idea)
- Organization
- Enthusiasm for the topic
- Tech knowledge

Digital Resources (same as for the previous idea)
- **Udemy:** The largest online website for selling courses (https://www.udemy.com/)
- **Teachable:** Online training site similar to Udemy (https://teachable.com/)
- **Create Awesome Online Courses:** This course taught by David Siteman Garland is a fantastic place to get started before you create your own course (https://www.createawesomeonlinecourses.com/)

22. Create & sell an information product

Difficulty: Medium
Profit Potential: Medium
Size of Opportunity: Large
Initial Cost: Low

What is it?
An information product can come in many formats. At the end of the day it has to help the buyer by solving a problem or providing some type of benefit, usually in the form of advice, a how-to guide or some type of resource toolkit.

Tim Ferriss speaks about the idea of selling information products often in his blog and in his remote worker bestseller, *The 4 Hour Work Week*. The intriguing thing about developing and selling an information product is that it doesn't require you to hold inventory or store goods in your basement. Information products take time and effort to develop, but once they've been created they become an asset that pays dividends far into the future. Information products also take longer to go out of date, and if you develop a system for selling these products you can end up building a solid multi-million dollar business very quickly.

How much can I make?
Depending on the type of product you sell, the sky's the limit on how much you can make on a single information product. Some consulting firms sell market research reports on specific industries for $5,000 or more per report, while some subscription consumer newsletters can be purchased for as little as $5 per issue.

I became fascinated with this idea since I realized the massive potential of developing an information product that helps people achieve results. For instance, consider how Melyssa Griffin created a multi-million-dollar business through her lifestyle blog by creating a series of informational courses on Pinterest. Or how the author Steven Scott has written 40+ books on Amazon and regularly makes over $40,000 per month in royalties. Informational products can be challenging to create, but once you have an idea for how to solve a specific problem for a set group of individuals you will be on the right track.

How do I start?
Before you get started with creating an information product, you've got to do some research. First, figure out your niche. Look at the type of people you want to serve and the problems they face on a regular basis. Do you have any knowledge that they can benefit from? If not, can you research the area to answer some of their pressing questions? Once you have that sorted, you need to figure out what format information product buyers in your niche prefer. Is it video, podcast, newsletter, online course, or ebook? Once you have this information, you can start creating your information product.

Skills Needed
- Writing ability
- Teaching or training experience
- Knowledge about a specific category

Digital Resources
- **The Balance Small Business:** "How to Make Money Selling Information Products Online" (https://www.thebalancesmb.com/sell-information-products-online-4129549)
- **StartupBros:** "9 Ways to Create an Information Product with Zero Expertise" (https://startupbros.com/9-ways-to-create-an-information-product-with-zero-expertise/)
- **Venture Harbour:** "7 Ways to Earn a Living Selling Ebooks, Courses, and Information Products Online" (https://www.ventureharbour.com/7-ways-to-sell-more-information-products/)

23. Create a membership subscription website

Difficulty: High
Profit Potential: High
Size of Opportunity: Medium
Initial Cost: Medium

What is it?
Similar to the idea of creating an information product, create a membership subscription website which helps people connect with one another or provides them with some kind of service which is hard to get somewhere else.

How much can I make?
If you create a membership site that charges users $5 per month for premium content or some type of value, you only need 400 subscribers to meet your $2,000 per month goal.

One of my favorite examples of this type of project is the website 750words.com. The website itself is designed to help individuals get over the hurdle of writing regularly. Many people want to create a regular writing habit, but few have the motivation to carry one day-after-day without some form of accountability.

The website 750words.com helps solve this problem by incentivizing people to write every day to maintain their "streak". The website allows you to create a profile and track your writing over time, and it charges a minimal $5 per month. With just over 4000 subscribers, we can calculate that the website is pulling in around $20,000 a month with very little overhead. The platform provides a niche service for a specific group (aspiring writers) and gives them an incentive for changing their behavior

How do I start?

Pick a niche that you can provide a service or solution to. Once you've identified a niche, find out what types of services, offerings or materials that niche would find beneficial. Would they benefit most from a forum to discuss a certain issue, or a series of videos? Would they like reports delivered to their email inbox or uploaded to the website? Think about these points as you start to create your membership website. You can use plugins for WordPress such as Memberful, website developers like Pedalo, or standalone tech services like Wild Apricot to set up your membership site and start processing payments right away.

Skills Needed
- WordPress and web design
- Marketing and SEO
- Organization

Digital Resources
- **The Membership Guys:** "How to Build a Membership Site in Under a Day" (https://www.themembershipguys.com/how-to-build-a-membership-in-a-day/)
- **Matthew Woodword:** "How to create a 6 figure membership site step by step" (https://www.matthewwoodward.co.uk/tutorials/start-profitable-membership-site-step-step/)
- **The Balance Small Business:** "How to Make Money at Home With a Membership Site" (https://www.thebalancesmb.com/making-money-at-home-with-a-membership-site-4153949)

24. Teach English online

Difficulty: Easy
Profit Potential: Medium
Size of Opportunity: Large
Initial Cost: Low

What is it?
If you are a native English speaker you can start earning money as an online language teacher. This job requires skyping with students (typically in other countries) who are looking to improve their English language speaking skills.

One of the major factors influencing an individual's ability to succeed in business and improve is their ability to communicate effectively with people. Part of this means being able to speak the same language as those you work with. Unfortunately for many people, major business languages like English and Chinese are their second languages. People all around the world are scrambling to learn English, and a great way to make money online is to tutor in English.

How much can I make?
VIPKID, a website that connects English speakers with children in China, says the average virtual English tutor earns approximately $2,000 per month. Tutors on the site make an average of $18 to $21 per hour, working on average about 25 hours per week. Not only that, many of the networks will provide you with course material and additional resources to make sure you provide the best tutoring possible.

How do I start?
There are over a dozen websites dedicated to connecting English language tutors with clients in places all around the world, and all you need to do to start is a solid internet connection and a webcam. You can apply to some of these networks in as little as an hour and be

verified in under a week. Once you become a tutor, you can provide training based on your availability.

Skills Needed
- English language fluency
- Teaching experience
- Patience

Digital Resources
- **VIP KID:** Teach English online to children in China for between $18 and $21 per hour (https://t.vipkid.com.cn/about)
- **Cambly:** Get paid about $10/hr to talk with adult English learners (https://www.cambly.com)
- **DadaABC:** Teach English online to children in China for minimum of 15 hours a week at $25/hr (https://www.dadaabc.com)

Arts & Entertainment (#25-29)

"Every child is an artist. The problem is how to remain an artist once we grow up."
Pablo Picasso

When we think about creative professions, we tend to think of the quintessential starving creative genius, typing away on a screenplay in the back of some cafe or working alone in a tiny studio on their next masterpiece. Artists are typically underpaid and struggling to make ends meet, yet there is a whole group of artists out there making big bucks selling their work online.

Here are a few ideas for those of you that have a creative streak.

25. Sell your art, designs, photography on online markets

Difficulty: Hard
Profit Potential: Low
Size of Opportunity: Small
Initial Cost: Low

What is it?
If you are an artist, find places to upload your art and market yourself. Sites like Etsy, Redbubble, and hundreds of others offer platforms for artists to post their physical and digital art online for others to purchase.

There is even a hybrid to this, with platforms that allow you to upload your art via digital channels which are then sold as physical products to customers (t-shirts, cups, coasters, etc.). While the money you may earn may not be enormous to start, the more art you put online, the more likely it will be that you reach your income threshold.

How much can I make?
Making a large amount of money online through sales of art and t-shirt designs on sites like Redbubble can be a challenge unless you are an expert marketer. This means that, while it may seem easy to upload your art to one of these sites, it may be more profitable to develop your own site and build connections within the global or local art community in order to make real money.

How do I start?
If you're a creative type, chances are you already have some ideas as to what type of artwork you'd like to sell. Start by experimenting and uploading a few pieces onto Redbubble to see if you gain any traction. It's also worthwhile looking at what other successful artists have done to market their work in this way.

Skills Needed
- Creativity
- Patience
- Marketing experience

Digital Resources
- **Redbubble:** Network of independent artists selling online (https://www.redbubble.com/)
- **Printful:** Custom print product drop shipping (https://www.printful.com/)
- **Zazzle:** Personalized and customized products (https://www.zazzle.com/)

26. Become a videographer or photographer

Difficulty: Medium
Profit Potential: Medium
Size of Opportunity: Medium
Initial Cost: Medium / High

What is it?
Sell your photography, videography and/or editing skills online. Digital video advertising is growing rapidly, and the demand for professionally shot and edited photos will never go away. Becoming a contract videographer or photographer is a great way to leverage your skills in the digital age.

How much can I make?
Photographers and videographers on Upwork can charge between $30 and $100 per hour depending on their level of expertise.

How do I start?
Start with the right equipment. Videography and photography both require special equipment and software. Depending on the type of niche you focus on, the equipment you need will also vary. Product videographers / photographers need a much different setup than people in the portrait and wedding niche. Next, be sure you have an online presence and a place to post your portfolios. People want to see what you've done in the past. Finally, go start looking for business. Use Upwork and Fiverr to build your portfolio and then look to expand with marketing of your personal website.

Skills Needed
- Photography / Videography experience
- Photo / Video editing
- Patience

Digital Resources
- **Digital Photography School:** Good resource for aspiring digital photography freelancers (https://digital-photography-school.com)
- **Valoso:** Videography job board (https://valoso.com)
- **Other freelance job boards:** Fiverr, Upwork, Guru.com, PeoplePerHour

27. Record voice overs and audiobooks

Difficulty: Medium
Profit Potential: High
Size of Opportunity: Medium
Initial Cost: Medium

What is it?
If you've ever been told you have a great voice, consider becoming a voice over freelancer for audiobooks and advertisements. The market for freelance voice over specialists is growing as more and more entrepreneurs and small business people are publishing ebooks and are creating videos for their businesses.

How much can I make?
Voiceover artists can make up to $50/hr doing voiceover work, though they typically charge per the number of works or the length of text.

How do I start?
Buy professional recording equipment (high end microphone and audio editing software) and then post your job on Fiverr and Upwork.

Skills Needed
- Comfortable speaking
- Audio engineering experience

Digital Resources
- **Damn Good Voices:** "Becoming a Voiceover Artist" (https://www.damngoodvoices.com/faq/BecomingAVoice)
- **ACX:** Network for voice over artists looking to record audiobooks (https://www.acx.com/)
- **Other networks:** Fiverr and Upwork

28. Become a social media (Instagram/Snapchat/YouTube) influencer

Difficulty: Hard
Profit Potential: Medium
Size of Opportunity: Medium
Initial Cost: Medium

What is it?
In an age where originality and content are valued above all else in viral marketing and advertising, the role that social media influencers play in driving purchase decisions among consumers has grown ever more important.

While this may seem like a fad, the digital ecosystem is not going away. If you aren't on one of these key social media platforms, this probably isn't for you. But if you have explored this area in the past, consider developing a strategy for growing your social media following and building a network of followers based on your content.

How much can I make?
The amount of money you can make as an influencer depends on the way that you monetize your following. Selling advertising through influencer networks may be a good way to get started, but the big money will be in creating one-to-one partnerships with big brands. You can also make money by including affiliate links in your posts or driving viewers to sign up to your newsletter (so you can monetize them later).

How do I start?
Building a large social media following can be a time intensive and hard process, but if you are dedicated you can build a following of 10,000+ in a specific niche in the space of a few months. With that type of following, you fall into the category of "micro influencer", and you can start to charge advertisers per post. At this point you will start receiving

offers which may equate to a few hundred or a few thousand dollars a month.

Skills Needed
- Creativity and originality
- Attention to detail
- Productiveness

Digital Resources
- **Scrunch:** Influencer marketing network (https://scrunch.com/)
- **Jenny Melrose:** "How to make money as an influencer" (https://jennymelrose.com/how-to-make-money-influencer/)
- **High Snobiety:** "Just How Much Do 'Influencers' Make?" (https://www.highsnobiety.com/p/how-much-do-influencers-make/)

29. Create a YouTube channel

Difficulty: Hard
Profit Potential: High
Size of Opportunity: Medium
Initial Cost: Medium

What is it?
Of all of the videos uploaded onto YouTube on a daily basis, only a small fraction of them will be viewed more than a few thousand times. Only a few YouTube stars ever make more than a few thousand per month in advertising revenue. Still, YouTube is one of the best ways to earn money that is out there. Why is that? Because YouTube remains one of the highest engagement areas to find potential customers for a product or idea. It is also the perfect delivery channel to make money through affiliate links, partnership deals or content marketing via on camera sponsorship arrangements.

How much can I make?
The number of content creators on YouTube making at least $100,000 a year has increased by 40% year over year in the last few years. That being said, these top tier content producers represent the exception, not the norm, and many YouTubers are making little money through advertising on the site. But if you use YouTube as a marketing channel to drive business to your website or affiliate links you stand a much better chance of reaching the $2,000 a month range.

How do I start?
Start by creating videos in a specific niche and start to test the market to see if there is any interest in what you have to say or talk about. Videos that are funny, have to do with travel, or teach the viewer something useful are more likely to get views than others. Check out a few resources like Creator Academy and Wikihow on the best way to approach creating a popular YouTube channel. According to YouTube,

the topics that tend to do best in terms of total views are comedy, entertainment, how-to and style, and gaming.

Skills Needed
- Videography and video editing
- Planning and productivity
- Productiveness

Digital Resources
- **YouTube Creator Academy:** YouTube online teaching resources for video creators (https://creatoracademy.youtube.com)
- **WikiHow:** "How to Earn Money on YouTube" (https://www.wikihow.com/Earn-Money-on-YouTube)
- **Influencer Marketing Hub:** Estimate what other YouTube channels make from advertising (https://influencermarketinghub.com)

Strategy (#30-35)

"However beautiful the strategy, you should occasionally look at the results."
Sir Winston Churchill

Sometimes leaders within an organization get so caught up with the day-to-day activities of running a "business" that they lose sight of their long-term objectives. The same happens with individuals that get so wrapped up in the "rat race" that they forget to occasionally reassess their long term objectives.

When companies and individuals lose sight of what their long-term objectives are they risk wasting time and missing out on opportunities to grow. Individuals that can help cut through the noise to identify high-level trends and define long-term objectives are invaluable. If you have an eye and a mind for strategy, consider how you might pursue one of these ideas.

30. Opinion research and customer surveys

Difficulty: High
Profit Potential: High
Size of Opportunity: Medium
Initial Cost: Medium

What is it?
The Internet has made it possible for anyone to launch a full-scale market research project. If you have the right knowledge and interest in a subject, you can design a questionnaire, launch a survey to a targeted list of respondents, gather data and uncover insights on the best way to interact with customers. Companies live and die by their customers.

The more an organization understands its customer, the better it will be able to develop products, market its services and ultimately increase business. If you have ever considered developing your skills as a market researcher, consider going down this route and launching a service which helps companies target their customers (or potential customers) and uncover insights about what makes them tick.

How much can I make?
Market researchers on Upwork charge between $35 and $90/hr for survey development and design. Some researchers charge per project. If you earn $35/hr you can work 15 hours a week and meet the $2,000 a month target.

How do I start?
Platforms like SurveyMonkey and Typeform are great tools for survey design which allow you to set up free trial accounts before signing up to a full service. If you aren't ready to fully dive into the world of market research but still want to make money in this area, consider becoming a member of a panel like Toluna, which sends surveys to respondents daily. These surveys allow you to accrue points which build up over

time. It may not be enough money to survive, but joining a service like this will let you start to see how surveys tend to be designed (and how much room for improvement there is in this space).

Skills Needed
- Analytical and critical thinking
- Statistics and data analysis
- Survey writing

Digital Resources
- **Careerlancer:** "How to be a Freelance Market Researcher" (https://careerlancer.net/freelance-market-researcher/)
- **Other resources:** search Upwork and Fiverr for "market research" and "customer survey" jobs

31. Business intelligence and analysis

Difficulty: Hard
Profit Potential: Medium
Size of Opportunity: Medium
Initial Cost: Low

What is it?
Companies need to stay up to date on what's going on in their industry in order to stay competitive. They need to be aware of emerging trends in their market as well as other markets to be able to determine what the next innovative product or service will be, and to see what their competitors are up to. If you are interested in business and like to learn about emerging trends in different industries, you can likely find work as a business intelligence analyst for startups and mid-sized firms looking to better understand their competition.

How much can I make?
Business analysts can earn between $50 and $100/hr for market and competitive assessments and trend reports. At $50/hr, that's about 10 hours of work a week to reach $2,000 a month.

How do I start?
Create a profile on Upwork and Fiverr and start applying to business intelligence jobs to build a portfolio. From there, expand your profile and reach out to businesses in your local area to see if they need any freelance business intelligence work.

Skills Needed
- Secondary and desk research
- Data analysis and data science
- Attention to detail

Digital Resources
- **Bridging the Gap:** "Becoming a Business Analyst" (http://www.bridging-the-gap.com/becoming-a-business-analyst/)
- **WikiHow:** "How to be a Business Analyst" (https://www.wikihow.com/Be-a-Business-Analyst)
- **Big Data Made Simple:** "Top Business Intelligence Tools in the Market" (http://bigdata-madesimple.com/top-business-intelligence-bi-tools-in-the-market/)

32. Business plan writing

Difficulty: Medium
Profit Potential: High
Size of Opportunity: Medium
Initial Cost: Low

What is it?
Business plan writers tend to have experience working within large organizations or small startups and are knowledgeable about what goes into making a successful business plan.

How much can I make?
Business plan writers tend to charge between $75 and $100 an hour on Upwork, or about 8 hours of work a week to hit the $2,000 a month mark.

How do I start?
Create a profile on Upwork and Fiverr and start building your profile. If you don't know a lot about what goes into a business plan, but you want to pursue this idea, you've got to be sure to do your research. People that hire business plan writers want to engage with experts, so you need to be sure you come across as one.

Skills Needed
- Expertise in a particular industry
- Understanding of finance and business principles
- Attention to detail

Digital Resources
- **BPlans.com:** Great resource for learning to write business plans (https://www.bplans.com)
- **WikiHow:** "How to write a business plan" (https://www.wikihow.com/Write-a-Business-Plan)

33. Innovation consulting

Difficulty: Hard
Profit Potential: High
Size of Opportunity: Medium
Initial Cost: Medium

What is it?
Innovation consulting is the process through which an individual or a team helps come up with new and innovative ways to improve a product, process or system to provide more value to the business and the customers. Typically the innovation consulting process involves the analysis of emerging trends and new products, brainstorming new ideas and concepts, and then the consolidation of new product ideas with existing business capabilities. This is a type of consulting that has grown popular in recent years because of the growing importance of innovation and the increase in competition across nearly every industry.

How much can I make?
On Upwork, the price range for innovation consultants is quite wide, from about $60 to $150/hr. Different experts promote themselves based on their backgrounds in different ways. If you're an author of a book on innovation, for instance, you're much more likely to be able to charge higher prices. At $60/hr you'd only have to work for about 8 hours a week to meet the $2,000 a month target.

How do I start?
Start by creating a profile on Upwork (innovation consulting isn't as popular of an idea on Fiverr). You can use your Upwork account to win a few jobs and create a portfolio for yourself. Because this type of consulting job relies on references for business growth, be sure you ask your clients for letters of recommendations and referrals for new business after you've worked with them.

The tricky part of this gig is to find the right customers willing to pay for your services. It is likely that you will have to find businesses that are less "cutting edge" and behind the times when it comes to technology. These are the ideal customers, because they are most likely to benefit from this type of engagement.

Skills Needed
- Design thinking and innovation framework expertise
- Business analysis and strategy background
- Public speaking and training experience

Digital Resources
- **The Muse:** "How to Break Into Innovation Consulting" (https://www.themuse.com/advice/how-to-break-into-innovation-consulting)
- **Board of Innovation:** "A week in the life of an Innovation Consultant" (https://www.boardofinnovation.com/blog/2018/04/16/a-week-in-the-life-of-an-innovation-consultant/)

34. Public relations

Difficulty: Medium
Profit Potential: High
Size of Opportunity: Medium
Initial Cost: Low

What is it?
Doing public relations or public affairs management through digital media channels can be a lucrative option for digital nomads looking to develop a steady income while working remotely. More and more people, companies and organizations are turning to digital media channels to increase their visibility and improve their brand, and they often need the help of PR professionals to drive engagement and tell the right stories about their businesses.

How much can I make?
Companies typically pay a business a monthly retainer (ranging anywhere from $2,000 per month to $5,000 per month) which takes into consideration an estimated hourly rate and the expectation of some type of results (articles, press clippings, etc.).

How do I start?
Public relations management requires various skill sets, but most frequently requires working with businesses and journalists to help create positive press for the company in question. Business models can take many forms, but the most common way that PR firms operate is this regular monthly retainer, followed by a la carte menu options for additional work such as branding, logo design, etc.

Skills Needed
- Emotional intelligence
- Research and copywriting
- Networking and negotiation

Digital Resources
- **Help a Reporter Out (HARO):** Online newsletter of press mention opportunities (https://www.helpareporter.com/)
- **Connectifier:** Great resource for identifying journalists in PR campaigns
- **Brandwatch:** "21 PR Tools and Resources" (https://www.brandwatch.com/blog/pr-tools-resources/)

35. Digital content marketing and brand consultant

Difficulty: Medium
Profit Potential: Medium
Size of Opportunity: High
Initial Cost: Low

What is it?
Digital content marketing and brand consultants work with companies to help them develop marketing strategies and activities which bring in more leads and drive sales online. Activities of a marketing consultant include things like strategic marketing plan development, content planning and creation, and brand message design.

How much can I make?
High earning marketing and brand consultants charge between $40 and $75/hr on Upwork. At $40/hr, a marketing consultant would need to work approximately 12 hours a week to hit the $2,000 a month mark.

This type of work is typically billed on a project basis or an hourly rate, and can bring in several hundred dollars a day depending on your skill set and level of experience. Most of this work can be done online and over the telephone. Some freelance marketing experts can earn up to $2,000 per client per month on a retainer basis.

How do I start?
One of the best ways to build a side business in this space is to create a name for yourself. If you don't have experience creating digital content or marketing campaigns for clients already, create an account on Upwork, Fiverr and any other online freelance platform you can find and start doing some work for them. Once you've made a few connections and hopefully gotten a few good reviews, create a website for yourself to advertise your services.

There are thousands of marketing specialists and strategists out there, but the market demand is growing so rapidly that if you are even slightly above average you will be able to make a comfortable side income for yourself in no time.

Skills Needed
- Writing and content creation
- Marketing and advertising knowledge
- Good communication

Digital Resources
- **Content Marketing Institute:** Fantastic resource for online content marketers (https://contentmarketinginstitute.com)
- **Digital Marketer:** Fantastic resource for digital marketing professionals (https://www.digitalmarketer.com/)
- **WikiHow:** "How to Become a Marketing Consultant" (https://www.wikihow.com/Become-a-Marketing-Consultant)

Operations (#36-43)

"Eat a live frog first thing in the morning and nothing worse will happen to you the rest of the day."
Mark Twain

Sometimes you have to do unpleasant work in order to make progress towards a goal or achieve something big. The ideas outlined in this chapter aren't incredibly exciting, sexy, or new, but they're always in demand and will get you paid if you're willing to put in the work.

If all you want to do is create a steady stream of income on the side of your current job and you don't mind doing something relatively monotonous or tedious, check out the ideas in this chapter. If not, skip over it, I won't be offended.

36. Data entry

Difficulty: Medium
Profit Potential: High
Size of Opportunity: Medium
Initial Cost: Low

What is it?
There is almost nothing exciting about the idea of doing data entry. That being said, data entry jobs are some of the steadiest around and you will be able to rely on work in this space for years to come. Data entry can also mean a lot of things, so be sure you know what you're getting yourself into when you apply to start working in one of these gigs.

For instance, it can require formatting raw data into a table or spreadsheet, pulling together customer information from a form and adding it to a database, or even researching a topic online and compiling that information online. If you can handle the periods of boredom required to collate raw data into spreadsheets, you will be pleasantly surprised to find out that there is a whole lot of work available to you online.

How much can I make?
Data entry freelancers on Upwork make between $25 and $40/hr. If you work 20 hours a week doing data entry at $25/hr, you can reach $2,000 a month.

How do I start?
Join Upwork and Fiverr and start bidding on projects. Because this type of skill is relatively commoditized, you will need to be fast when applying to job postings that require this skill. It's also work reaching out to law firms and market research companies in your local area to see if they're looking for freelance data entry professionals.

Skills Needed
- Attention to detail
- Fast typing
- Patience

Digital Resources
- **WikiHow:** "How to Work from Home With Data Entry" (https://www.wikihow.com/Work-from-Home-With-Data-Entry)
- **The Balance Careers:** "Best Data Entry Jobs from Home" (https://www.thebalancecareers.com/legitimate-data-entry-jobs-from-home-3542500)

37. Become a translator or do translation related services

Difficulty: Medium
Profit Potential: High
Size of Opportunity: Medium
Initial Cost: Low

What is it?
More and more people are travelling, working internationally, and looking for opportunities to learn and communicate with others around the world. If you have a flair for language or even took basic French or Spanish in school, you may be able to work as a translator in one capacity or another. While apps that translate between languages are becoming ubiquitous, there is still a big need for human translation services, especially when it comes to document translation of more niche topic areas.

How much can I make?
On Upwork, you can typically earn anywhere from $30 to $40/hr translating and proofreading content from language to another. You would need to translate for about 17 hours a week to hit the $2,000 a month target. On translation websites like Unbabel and Gengo, editors make on average between $300 and $400 per month, lower than the target.

How do I start?
While you may consider looking on Upwork or Fiverr for translation businesses, the best place to start may be looking for work through an existing translation provider. Unbabel and Gengo are two online translation services which blend technology and human translation services together to provide high-level translation for enterprise clients. As a translator, all you need to do to work with one of these companies is pass a few language tests and then start receiving monthly payments for the translations you do.

Skills Needed
- Foreign language
- Spelling and grammar
- Fast typing

Digital Resources
- **Gengo:** Online language translation (https://gengo.com/)
- **Unbabel:** Computer / human assisted translation service (https://unbabel.com/)

38. Project manager

Difficulty: High
Profit Potential: Medium
Size of Opportunity: Medium
Initial Cost: Low

What is it?
Project management is managing the specific timeline and deliverables associated with a specific project within a set timeframe and set of parameters. When you look up project management on Upwork, you will find dozens of project managers with expertise in everything from business development to strategic planning, operations to IT. If you have attention to detail and like working with people, this may be the job for you.

How much can I make?
Project managers typically charge between $50-75/hr. If you spend 20 hours a week project managing, that equates to approximately $4,000 per month. Some more experienced project managers can earn up to $120/hr.

How do I start?
Consider looking at the website TheDigitalProjectManager.com for resources or the Project Management Institute (PMI.org) for resources and information on how best to develop a virtual project management business. While this isn't the sexiest of digital nomad jobs, it pays the bills and can provide great security. The world will always need organized and detail-oriented people who are good at project management and communicating with teams.

Skills Needed
- Organization
- Attention to detail
- Management experience

Digital Resources
- **The Digital Project Manager:** Great blog for digital project managers (https://thedigitalprojectmanager.com/project-management-skills/)
- **ProjectManager.com:** A great resource for project management tips (https://www.projectmanager.com/blog/project-management-skills)
- **Various Courses:** Available on Udemy, YouTube and LinkedIn Learning

39. Product management

Difficulty: Medium
Profit Potential: High
Size of Opportunity: Medium
Initial Cost: Low

What is it?
Product management is similar to project management, but rather than focusing on the success of a specific project, being a product manager requires ensuring the continuous success of an entire product. Product management requires a long-term vision and focuses more on the "why" and "what" of a product rather than the "how".

How much can I make?
Experienced product managers can make between $75 and $150/hr on Upwork. At $75 per hour you can work 7 hours a week to make the $2,000 a month target. Experienced product managers typically work with clients on a project by project basis for long-term projects rather than in short engagements.

How do I start?
To start working as a freelance product manager, you need to get your name out there. Start writing about topics related to product management on Quora and Medium. From there, start looking for Upwork jobs on Fiverr, Upwork and online directories like Product Manager HQ. Start building your portfolio with smaller jobs and move up to larger engagements.

Skills Needed
- Highly organized
- Collaborative
- Strategic and persistent

Digital Resources
- **Product Manager HQ:** Database of freelance product management jobs (https://jobs.productmanagerhq.com/)
- **ProdPad:** "How to Become a Product Manager With No Experience" (https://www.prodpad.com/blog/steps-to-becoming-a-product-manager/)
- **Koombea:** "The Difference Between Product and Project Management" (https://www.koombea.com/blog/the-difference-between-product-and-project-management/)

40. Executive virtual assistant

Difficulty: Medium
Profit Potential: High
Size of Opportunity: Medium
Initial Cost: Low

What is it?
If you're organized, and you like scheduling meetings, booking travel and generally helping manage the day-to-day activities of a business, consider going down the route of being an executive virtual assistant. Being an executive virtual assistant means working with an executive or a small business owner to sort out all the logistics of a business, from arranging appointments to booking travel and accommodation.

How much can I make?
Experienced virtual assistants in the U.S. and Europe can make between $35 and $45 an hour, meaning if you work approximately 20 hours a week as a VA you can make $2,000 per month.

How do I start?
Create a profile for yourself on Upwork and Fiverr and indicate that you are available to work as a virtual assistant. You may be more likely to get work if you price your time around $25/hr to start off and then ramp up as you get more experience.

Skills Needed
- Expertise with office management tech (i.e. MS Office, Wordpress, Freshbooks, QuickBooks, CRM systems, Asana, Slack)
- Fast learner
- Well organized

Digital Resources
- **Peopleperhour.com:** Directory for freelance virtual assistant jobs (https://www.peopleperhour.com)
- **Upwork**
- **Fiverr**

41. Transcribing

Difficulty: Easy
Profit Potential: Low
Size of Opportunity: Medium
Initial Cost: Low

What is it?
Transcribing of interviews can be a tedious task, but you can earn about $20-30 per hour transcribing if you are fast at typing and make very few errors.

How much can I make?
At $30/hr, you would need to work about 17 hours per week to reach the $2,000 a month mark.

How do I start?
Go on Fiverr and Upwork, create an account and start applying to jobs. It's also worthwhile reaching out to law firms and market research companies which may be looking for transcribers to assist on longer term projects. This type of work can be monotonous, but if you find the right client the work will be steady, and you may be able to arrange for a higher hourly rate.

Skills Needed
- Fast and accurate typing
- Attention to detail
- Good time management

Digital Resources
- **Express Scribe:** Audio player software for PC or Mac designed to help transcribe audio (https://www.nch.com.au/scribe/)
- **Freemake Audio / Video Converter:** For changing video and audio file types (http://www.freemake.com)
- **Dragon Dictation:** The world's best known automatic audio transcription software (https://www.nuance.com)

42. Interviewing experts for money

Difficulty: Medium
Profit Potential: Medium
Size of Opportunity: Medium
Initial Cost: Medium

What is it?
Did you know you can get paid for interviewing people? Making money by interviewing people can be a fantastic way to make a little bit of money on the side. There are various ways you can actually make money from interviewing people, but the general idea is that you find and reach out to experts in a certain niche and get them to speak with you on the record about a certain topic. From there, you can sell access to those interviews through a subscription or membership website, or you can create an information product from the expert advice.

How much can I make?
The amount of money you will make from this gig depends on your method for monetizing the interviews. Andrew Warner of Mixergy created a website that aggregates expert interviews and courses on various topics related to entrepreneurship. He offers a lot of content for free on his website, but then puts a portion of it behind a paywall. He charges $49 per month for full access to courses and interviews, or $399 per year in a lump sum. With a similar pricing model you would need to attract about 40 subscribers to hit the $2,000 per month mark.

How do I start?
You can then use these interviews to make money in a variety of ways. For instance, you can use the interview material to attract readers and then advertise your own products. You can post interviews with experts and then link to affiliate links to make money when people buy products linked from the site.

Another way to make money is to try to secure interviews with top name executives and experts and then try to sell those interviews to publications for a fee. Finally, you can work with companies that are interested in getting an expert perspective on certain topics. You can then contact these experts and interview them based on an agreed upon fee with the client.

A good place to start is to identify a niche that you are interested in and then reach out to experts in that niche to ask for interviews. Once they agree to be interviewed, record, record, record! The more value you can capture in this way, the more you'll be able to hone your interviewing skills and make more money in the long run.

Skills Needed
- Emotional intelligence
- Curiosity and creativity
- Well organized

Digital Resources
- **Create Awesome Interviews:** This course run by David Siteman Garland is a great overview of what it takes to create a profitable interview business (https://www.createawesomeinterviews.com/)
- **Mixergy:** Check out the Mixergy site for some inspiration on how to monetize an expert interview side hustle (https://mixergy.com)

43. User testing

Difficulty: Easy
Profit Potential: Small
Size of Opportunity: Small
Initial Cost: Low

What is it?
User experience testers, also sometimes referred to as quality assurance (QA) testers help companies review their websites and offer advice on redesigns to specific products or solutions. If you are someone who is frequently frustrated by website usability and are looking for an opportunity to voice your frustrations for a fee, look no further than this gig. As a user tester, you visit company's websites and give your feedback about the user experience.

How much can I make?
On average you can make about $10 per website review. Each review requires around 20 minutes of screen capture and voiceover, followed by a few written response questions. Chances are, it will be hard to reach the $2,000 per month mark with this type of work but based on how easy it is to make money in this way you might as well.

How do I start?
There are lots of websites out there that allow you to join their panel to conduct user experience tests do this in a simple and straightforward way. Some of my favorites include usertesting.com and respondent.io. You can also post your QA jobs on Fiverr and Upwork if you are looking to expand your reach.

Skills Needed
- Good communication
- Fast worker
- Flexibility

Digital Resources
- **Usertesting.com:** Great site for quick user testing projects (https://www.usertesting.com)
- **Respondent.io:** Be a respondent on user testing projects across a variety of topics (https://app.respondent.io)
- **Workathomewoman.com:** Fantastic list of user testing websites (https://www.theworkathomewoman.com/test-websites/)

Writing (#44-50)

"We are all apprentices in a craft where no one ever becomes a master."
Ernest Hemingway

Writing is an art and a science. It is a passion and a profession. It is a blessing and a curse. Once bitten by the writing bug it may be hard to cut the habit.

If you want to make a living from writing, there are a whole host of options open to you. The tricky thing is to decide what you want to focus on and then dive in with everything you've got.

44. Write a niche consumer newsletter

Difficulty: Medium
Profit Potential: Medium
Size of Opportunity: Medium
Initial Cost: Low

What is it?
If you are looking for a project that can be scaled quickly and could lead to massive returns in the long run, consider developing information products or newsletters which can be sold as a subscription to people in a certain niche or interest area.

How much can I make?
Consumer focused subscription newsletters can go for anything from $5 per issue to $199 per year (about $16 per issue) and above. If you sell $5 in subscriptions you'll have to get 400 subscribers before you reach your $2,000 a month mark. The good news is, once you've hit this point, you will regularly be making $2,000 a month with very little effort on your part (besides writing the actual letter).

How do I start?
Start by measuring interest in a certain topic or area of focus. This may mean creating a free report or some kind of guide related to the newsletter you're thinking of creating and then offering to give it away for free in exchange for someone's email address. FOCUS ON DELIVERING VALUE TO THE READER. Once you've validated an idea you can start planning out your subscription newsletter. You can create a paid subscription newsletter on your own, or you can use a tool like Memberful or Substack to do the hard work of managing payments for you.

Skills Needed
- WordPress and Mailchimp (or other web marketing service)
- Writing
- Scheduling and project management

Digital Resources
- **Memberful:** Site for creating paid subscription membership sites and newsletters (https://memberful.com/)
- **Substack:** Website for creating and monetizing your own paid subscription newsletter (https://www.substack.com/)
- **ChargeBee SaaS Blog:** "Subscription Business Model Series - Email Newsletters" (https://www.chargebee.com/blog/subscription-business-model-series-newsletter/)

45. Write a niche industry newsletter

Difficulty: Hard
Profit Potential: Medium
Size of Opportunity: Medium
Initial Cost: Low

What is it?
This is very similar to the previous idea. Suffice it to say, paid newsletters are coming back into fashion in a big way. If you have experience in a certain industry and feel you would be able to provide value to those in that industry through a carefully curated newsletter, consider going down the path of creating a free or paid industry newsletter.

How much can I make?
Depending on your content and the size of your niche, you can easily hit the mark for selling $2,000 worth of subscriptions. Small and medium sized businesses (SMBs) are more likely to spend money on industry newsletters that help them get ahead of the competition. Consider a monthly subscription cost somewhere between $30 and $100, depending on the length and detail in the report. With a $30 fee, you only have to sell about 70 subscriptions to meet the $2,000 per month mark.

How do I start?
Focus on making the value extremely clear to the client and your customers will have no trouble spending up to $100 on a targeted newsletter. Create a format and a structure for the newsletter so that you can crank out each report on a regular basis without too much effort. Then create a landing page website and start asking people for sign-ups. You'll likely want to consider driving traffic through social media or Google ads to ramp up subscriptions.

Skills Needed
- WordPress and Mailchimp (or other web marketing service)
- Writing
- Scheduling and project management

Digital Resources
- **Memberful:** Site for creating paid subscription membership sites and newsletters (https://memberful.com/)
- **Substack:** Website for creating and monetizing your own paid subscription newsletter (https://www.substack.com/)
- **ChargeBee SaaS Blog:** "Subscription Business Model Series - Email Newsletters" (https://www.chargebee.com/blog/subscription-business-model-series-newsletter/)

46. Freelance blogging

Difficulty: Medium
Profit Potential: High
Size of Opportunity: Medium
Initial Cost: Low

What is it?
The market is growing for content marketers, and there will always be a space for bloggers interested in writing about various topics online. Depending on your skillset, you may be able to pick a niche area and secure regular freelance blogging jobs to ghost write for websites in your specific area of expertise.

How much can I make?
Content writer fees vary greatly but based on a review of highly scored bloggers on Upwork and Fiverr the range seems to be between $35 and $75 per hour. This means that even at $35 per week you would be able to hit the $2,000 mark by working approximately 15 hours per week.

How do I start?
Create accounts on Upwork and Fiverr right away. Also check out the ProBlogger jobs board and FreelanceWritingGigs.com for ideas on where to find blogging projects.

Skills Needed
- Writing
- Creativity
- Attention to detail

Digital Resources
- **Upwork**
- **Fiverr**

- **Freelance Writing Gigs:** Great resource for writing jobs (https://www.freelancewritinggigs.com/)
- **ProBlogger Jobs:** Directory for blogging jobs (https://problogger.com/jobs/)
- **The Balance Small Business:** "9 Places to Find Paid Blogging Jobs" (https://www.thebalancesmb.com/top-places-to-find-paid-blogging-jobs-2531559)

47. Freelance copywriting

Difficulty: Medium
Profit Potential: Medium
Size of Opportunity: Medium
Initial Cost: Low

What is it?
Every single profession and niche needs people that are able to write interesting and engaging copy. Freelance writers can be paid per individual article or piece, or they can be kept on retainer to support a business for any of their writing needs. If you are a strong writer and find writing in an engaging way fun and easy, chances are you would make a fantastic freelance copywriter.

How much can I make?
Copywriters may charge on a per page or per hour basis. Most copywriters can earn anywhere from $50 to $100 per hour and easily make $2,000 to $5,000 a month.

How do I start?
Great places to look for work in this area include Upwork or Craigslist. There are also ways to develop this skill by simply reaching out to people in your community and asking them if they need help with writing content for their business, blog, or other endeavour.

Skills Needed
- Writing
- Creativity
- Attention to detail

Digital Resources
- **Various courses:** Available on LinkedIn Learning, YouTube and Udemy
- **Copyblogger:** A great source for learning how to hone your copywriting (https://www.copyblogger.com/copywriting-101/)

48. Start a lifestyle blog in a specific niche

Difficulty: High
Profit Potential: High
Size of Opportunity: Medium
Initial Cost: Low

What is it?
Imagine if you could make over $50,000 per month writing about your favorite recipes and foods? That's exactly what Lindsay Mostrom does with her food blog Pinch of Yum. Lindsay is a former 4th grade teacher who decided to start Pinch of Yum seven years ago and has grown it into a six figure business which allows her to travel the world (or stay at home) whenever she wants.

If you know a lot about a specific topic or are just passionate about something, why not start writing a blog which helps and teaches others about that niche?

How much can I make?
According to ProBlogger, a well-respected resource for bloggers trying to make money from their sites, only about 13% of bloggers trying to make money from their blogs make over $1,000 per month.

How do I start?
Successful blogging requires a concise plan and a strategy for monetizing your blog quickly. Apart from that, the best way to start a blog is to outline what you want to write about and just start! A few fantastic sites to go to for inspiration and guidance on how to start and monetize your blog include Smart Blogger and Createandgo. While there are countless articles on the topic of making money by blogging, the real key is to start. Action wins every time, and the more time you spend thinking about blogging, the less likely you will be to start it.

Skills Needed
- Writing
- Creativity
- Planning and time management

Digital Resources
- **Pro Blogger:** The home for bloggers wanting to create and grow their blogs (https://problogger.com/)
- **Smart Blogger:** One of my favorite blogs on how to blog (https://smartblogger.com/)
- **Createandgo:** Great information and courses on how to make money blogging (https://createandgo.co/)
- **LifeHacker:** "Can I really make a living by blogging" (https://lifehacker.com/can-i-really-make-a-living-by-blogging-1537783554)

49. Start a travel blog

Difficulty: Hard
Profit Potential: High
Size of Opportunity: Medium
Initial Cost: High

What is it?
Some people just seem to have it all. They travel the world, post videos and images of their trips, and they make money while doing it! A quick search online for travel bloggers comes back with over 12 million results, and there are dozens of individual travel-centric Instagram influencers with over 500,000 followers.

If this sounds appetizing (why wouldn't it) then think about launching your own travel blog. It may be easier than you think.

How much can I make?
According to a blog post on the Instagram plugin site Later, "One travel blogger and photographer with 108K followers and a 9.2% engagement rate listed their content creation at up to $1000 per Instagram Post, $1200 per Instagram Post + Blog Post, $200 per Instagram Story and $2,000-$5,000 for a 60-Second Product Video."

You probably won't start off making that kind of money, but based on a review of other earnings estimates from travel bloggers, it may be realistic to assume you would be able to pull in between $2,000 and $5,000 per month from blogging and other writing activities.

How do I start?
For many of us, the idea of being a travel writer is something that is infinitely appealing, yet few of us have the faintest idea of how to start a successful travel blog website which will support our lifestyles. One of the main challenges associated with launching a travel blog is that, in

order to start travelling (and blogging), you need to have money. One way to get around this is to have another side gig or business to support you before your travel blogging takes off.

At the end of the day, the best way to get started is just to launch a blog and get writing. Go to other travel blogger sites you find interesting and try to mirror their content. Go ask questions and do your research about how they get sponsors and advertising deals. Be open and explore!

Skills Needed
- The travel bug
- Creative writing
- Networking and collaboration

Digital Resources
- **Expert Vagabond:** "11 Secrets to Becoming a Professional Travel Blogger" (https://expertvagabond.com/professional-travel-blogger/)
- **Goats on the Road:** "How Much Money Can You Make From a Travel Blog?" (https://www.goatsontheroad.com/much-can-make-travel-blog/)
- **Nomadic Matt:** "9 ways to become a successful blogger" (https://www.nomadicmatt.com/travel-blogs/become-successful-travel-blogger/)

50. Write an eBook

Difficulty: Medium
Profit Potential: Medium
Size of Opportunity: Medium
Initial Cost: Low

What is it?
If you are a writer or you've always wanted to be, consider trying your hand at writing an eBook or two and publishing it on Amazon as a Kindle book. This is a great option for someone who wants to develop a second stream of income but doesn't want to go through the process of creating an entire business from scratch. Writing an eBook doesn't have to take a lot of time, in fact you don't even have to write the book yourself.

How much can I make?
It's hard to predict how much money you'll be able to make writing eBooks on Amazon. Some books may sell between 100 and 150 copies per month. At $0.99, that's about $148 per month. So how do you get to $2,000 per month? By writing lots of books. This idea takes time to implement, and there is loads of reading you can do online about the best way to start a kindle publishing business.

How do I start?
Start by picking a specific niche topic which seems to have a lot of readers. Ideally this is a niche or a topic you know something about, otherwise you'll have to spend some time researching the topic (or hiring someone to do this for you). Next you have to write the book and post it on the KDP (Kindle Direct Publishing) website.

Skills Needed
- Writing ability
- Persistence
- Patience

Digital Resources
- **Udemy:** There are great courses available to help you learn more about how to start a successful KDP business
- **KindlePreneur:** Dave Chesson runs the site KindlePreneur and has a TON of great articles on the topic of launching books successfully (https://kindlepreneur.com/)
- **UpFuel:** "How much money can one kindle book make?" (https://upfuel.com/how-much-money-can-one-kindle-book-make-1-year-case-study/)

Online Money Making Tools & Resources [Bonus Section]

Remote jobs

Remote.co: Remote.co was founded by Sarah Sutton Fell and is a fantastic resource for businesses and individuals looking to learn more about remote work. The remote.co site provides a long list of curated remote working jobs broken out by topic, industry and specialty area. They have jobs in categories such as customer service, HR, sales & development. The site also has loads of information on best practices around how to grow and lead a remote team. Jobs are searchable across multiple areas of focus including HR, design, IT, project management and writing. Most jobs are contract or commission based.

Remote OK: Remote OK was developed as a side project by Pieter Levels. It's a site that helps people find remote jobs by seniority level, industry and role type. Currently the site has approximately 30,000 job posts across various industries and areas of expertise. There are job postings for everything from app design to online teaching and non-technical writing work. The site has a clean design which makes looking for jobs super straightforward. Job postings typically require you to apply through a company website once you click through to view the job description. Pieter Levels is also the creator of Nomad List, a database of crowd sourced information on international cities based on their attractiveness as a digital nomad location.

We Work Remotely: WeWorkRemotely.com is the world's largest site for sourcing remote work opportunities across various skill sets and areas of expertise. You can search by various categories like development, programming, copywriting and design. Businesses must pay $299 to post a job on the site, which keeps the quality of job postings high. The site is part sponsored by the authors of the book Remote by 37Signals co-founders.

Remotive.io: The mission of Remotive is to help users "find their dream job online". The Remotive website attracts over 100,000 readers per month and is constantly updating its list of job posts. You can also sign up for the site's bi-monthly newsletter with job listings delivered straight to your inbox. Jobs can be found in everything from education to engineering and marketing.

Virtual Vocations: Virtual Vocations has built up a network of over 11,000 companies which work with and hire remote employees. Each company is vetted ahead of time, making the likelihood of finding a legitimate remote job more likely. The company also provides free courses on how to get the most out of working remotely (in fact they cover everything from how to set up the proper virtual resume to how to develop telecommuting work proposals).

Working Nomads: Working Nomads delivers a curated list of jobs to your inbox weekly or monthly.

Jobscribe: Jobscribe sends you a daily email with remote job listings at tech startups.

WFH.io: WFH.io (for Work From Home) is a website that focuses on remote digital and tech jobs in product management, software development and marketing.

Outsourcely: Outsourcely pairs remote workers with employees seeking full or part-time work.

Jobspresso: Jobspresso offers a curated list of over 1,000 jobs targeted towards remote workers. Jobs tend to be focused on software development and tech.

Freelance jobs

Upwork: Once called O-desk / Elance, Upwork is a globally recognize freelance platform where individuals can post jobs and make proposals for work. The site has grown in popularity in recent years, making it more challenging to become a certified freelancer. Make sure you have a strong resume and a niche skill when you apply, as all accounts are reviewed before they become active.

Toptal Business: Toptal Business was built after the company Toptal acquired Skillbridge, the elite freelancer site. Toptal Business is focused on helping the top 3% of freelancers to find interesting and fulfilling remote freelance work.

Fiverr: Fiver (with two r's) is a site where you post small jobs (typically for $5 each). The jobs can include add on's to increase the value of the project, and it is often a great place to start working online to develop a strong portfolio.

Guru: Guru allows freelancers to post portfolios of their work and be contacted by individuals look to hire designers and programmers.

Freelancer.com: Allows business owners to post jobs online and then freelancers can bid on them. With over 13 million users, this site is often one of the best places to go to look for steady freelance employment.

FreelancerMap.com: Freelancer Map allows you to search for thousands of remote IT projects on a contract basis.

PowertoFly: Helps match women in tech with work from anywhere jobs.

Dribbble: This site was created for designers to post their portfolios and find remote / anywhere jobs.

AngelList: Startup job posts for people, tick the box for "remote ok" jobs.

A Big Thank You

Before you go, I'd like to say thank you for purchasing this book.

I know you could have picked up any of the dozens out there on success and online money making, but you took a chance on mine.

Since you've gotten this far, I've got a small favor to ask.

Could you please take a minute to leave a review for this book on Amazon?

This feedback will help me continue to write the types of books that will help you and others get results. And if you loved it, then please let me know!

Best,
McVal

Printed in Great Britain
by Amazon